Black History

Contemporary Achievements

By Rebecca Szulhan

AV² provides enriched content that supplements and complements this book. Weigl's AV² books strive to create inspired learning and engage young minds in a total learning experience.

Go to www.av2books.com, and enter this book's unique code.

BOOK CODE

V459322

AV² by Weigl brings you media enhanced books that support active learning.

Download the AV² catalog at **www.av2books.com/catalog**

Your AV² Media Enhanced books come alive with...

Audio
Listen to sections of the book read aloud.

Key Words
Study vocabulary, and complete a matching word activity.

Video
Watch informative video clips.

Quizzes
Test your knowledge.

Embedded Weblinks
Gain additional information for research.

Slide Show
View images and captions, and prepare a presentation.

Try This!
Complete activities and hands-on experiments.

... and much, much more!

AV² Online Navigation on page 48

Published by AV² by Weigl
350 5th Avenue, 59th Floor
New York, NY 10118

Website: www.av2books.com www.weigl.com

Library of Congress Cataloging-in-Publication Data

Szulhan, Rebecca.
Contemporary achievements / Rebecca Szulhan.
p. cm. -- (Black history)
Includes index.
Summary: "Celebrates contemporary achievements of African Americans from the 1950s to the 2010s in all aspects of American culture, including the arts, sports, politics, and the sciences. Intended for fifth to eighth grade students"--Provided by publisher.
ISBN 978-1-62127-192-5 (hardcover : alk. paper) -- ISBN 978-1-62127-198-7 (softcover : alk. paper)
1. African Americans--History--Juvenile literature. 2. African Americans--Biography--Juvenile literature. I. Title.
E185.96.S983 2013
973'.0496073--dc23
2012040640

Printed in the United States of America in North Mankato, Minnesota
1 2 3 4 5 6 7 8 9 0 17 16 15 14 13 12

112012
WEP301112

Weigl acknowledges Getty Images as its primary image supplier for this title.

Editor: Heather Kissock
Designer: Terry Paulhus

Contents

Rising Above

African Americans have a long history in the United States of America. Their story began centuries ago, when they were first brought as slaves to the Americas. Although slavery was **abolished** in the mid-1800s, African Americans continued to face obstacles. Despite having their freedom, they had to struggle for equality. During the 1950s and 1960s, the **Civil Rights Movement** led to changes in American society and politics. African Americans were recognized as citizens of the United States. Over the years, African Americans have made important contributions to society in many fields, including politics, science, and film.

The important role African Americans have played in the history of the United States is recognized through events such as **Kwanzaa**, the celebration of African harvest, and **Black History Month**, celebrating African **heritage**. As well, in 1978, the United States Postal Service began issuing a Black Heritage series of stamps featuring prominent African Americans. Books, television programs, and other media have been produced focusing on the experiences of African Americans.

Despite the hurdles they have faced, many African Americans have had many great achievements. They have influenced all aspects of American culture, including the arts, sports, politics, and the sciences.

The U.S. Postal Service issued a Black Heritage series of stamps. In 2001, Roy Wilkins, executive director of the NAACP, was featured on one of these stamps.

David Blackwell

The 1950s

During the 1950s, African Americans made strides in many fields, including **academics**, television programming, literature, theater, and sports. It was a decade of many "firsts" for African Americans who were entering mainstream American culture for the first time.

Many African Americans broke ground and paved the way for others to achieve great success. For example, in 1952, Frank E. Petersen, Jr. became the Marine Corps' first African American aviator. Two years later, David Blackwell became the first African American to hold a permanent position at a major university. In 1955, contralto Marian Anderson became the first African American prima donna at the Metropolitan Opera Company in New York.

Gwendolyn Brooks Wins Pulitzer Prize

Gwendolyn Brooks won the Pulitzer Prize for poetry in 1950 for her book called *Annie Allen*. This recognition made her the first African American to win a Pulitzer Prize.

Gwendolyn Elizabeth Brooks was born June 7, 1917, in Topeka, Kansas. She grew up in Chicago, Illinois. The atmosphere in her house was warm and loving. Gwendolyn's parents encouraged her love of words from an early age, reading stories to her and her brother Dale when they were children. They often allowed her to write instead of doing her chores.

By the time Gwendolyn was 16 years old, 75 of her poems had been published. She graduated from Wilson Junior College with an English degree in 1936 and, two years later, married Henry Blakely. After briefly working as a cleaning woman and a secretary, Gwendolyn became the director of the local National Association for the Advancement of Colored People (NAACP) Youth Council. Her first collection of poetry, *A Street in Bronzeville*, was published in 1945. *Annie Allen* was published four years later. The poems in this collection tell the story of a woman's life and her struggle to overcome **racism** and poverty.

In addition to the Pulitzer Prize, Gwendolyn received many other honors. She has been inducted into the National Women's Hall of Fame and was chosen as the National Endowment for the Humanities Jefferson Lecturer, one of the highest honors for American literature

CONTEMPORARY QUICK FACTS

In 1968, Gwendolyn became the poet laureate for Illinois.

Gwendolyn Brooks was inducted into the National Women's Hall of Fame in 1988.

John F. Kennedy invited Gwendolyn to read at a Library of Congress poetry festival in 1962.

Gwendolyn Brooks died, pen in hand, on December 3, 2000, in her Chicago home. She was 83.

writers and the highest award in the humanities given by the federal government. Gwendolyn was also the keynote speaker for the Third Annual Kaw Valley Girl Scout Council Women of Distinction Banquet and String of Pearls, where she encouraged other aspiring poets to pursue their craft.

Lorraine Hansberry

Lorraine Hansberry is best known for writing the first Broadway play by an African American woman, *A Raisin in the Sun*. Born on May 19, 1930, in Chicago, Illinois, she was raised in a neighborhood made up mostly of people of European ancestry. She was often **discriminated** against, and her family was attacked by neighbors.

In 1956, after working at an African American newspaper in New York City, Hansberry decided to focus on her own writing. She wanted to write about the social experiences of African Americans in a realistic way. Often, she drew on events in her own life. *The Crystal Stair*, a play about a struggling African American family in Chicago, was her first major project. Later, it was renamed *A Raisin in the Sun*.

Starring Sidney Poitier, Claudia McNeil, and Ruby Dee, *A Raisin in the Sun* made its Broadway debut in 1959. It had 530 performances over two years. Hansberry received the New York Critic's Circle Award for the play and became the first African American and the youngest person to be given this award. In 1961, Poitier starred in the film version of *A Raisin in the Sun*, which won awards at the Cannes Film Festival in France.

In 1964, Hansberry wrote *The Movement: Documentary of a Struggle for Equality*. That same year, *The Sign in Sidney Bustein's Window*, her second play, opened on Broadway. Hansberry died the following year. A collection of her letters, writing, and interviews, *To Be Young, Gifted, and Black: Lorraine Hansberry in Her Own Words*, was published after her death.

A Raisin in the Sun

A *Raisin in the Sun* tells the story of the Younger family, who live in a one-room apartment in South Side, Chicago. One day, Mrs. Younger receives a check for $10,000 from her husband's life insurance policy. With this money, she buys a larger house in a better neighborhood. The local community association unsuccessfully attempts to buy back the Youngers' house to prevent an African American family from living in their neighborhood.

In 1973, *A Raisin in the Sun* was developed into an award-winning musical. For her role in the musical, Phylicia Rashad became the first African American actress to win a Best Actress Tony Award.

The 1960s

The 1960s were a time of change. People demanded **social reform**. The first **sit-ins** were held at school campuses, where students protested **segregation** at lunch counters. Soon, people held read-ins at libraries, stand-ins at movie theaters, and kneel-ins at churches. Other forms of protest were **boycotts**, pickets, and marches.

Dr. Martin Luther King, Jr. became an inspirational leader of the Civil Rights Movement. He sought change through peaceful means. Civil rights **activists** were successful, and a bill was passed so that all people would be treated equally. The first African American justice of the Supreme Court was appointed during the 1960s. This meant that African Americans could help enforce the law.

The 1960s were important years for space research and travel. On July 20, 1969, about 600 million people

Martin Luther King, Jr. was one of many civil rights leaders to inspire change.

watched their televisions as Neil Armstrong took his first step on the Moon. This was the beginning of the space exploration era. African Americans were closely involved in the research that helped missions into space succeed.

Jackie Robinson Joins the Dodgers

Another important milestone in the 1960s was the induction of Jackie Robinson into the Baseball Hall of Fame in 1962. During his trailblazing career, Jackie played in the World Series six times and helped the Brooklyn Dodgers win the series in 1955.

The future baseball legend was born in Cairo, Georgia, in 1919, as John Roosevelt Robinson. He was one of the first African Americans living in the South to play on a baseball team with children of European ancestry.

Although African Americans had excelled in individual sports, many people thought that they should not be allowed to play on a team with players of European ancestry. When Jackie played his first game with the Dodgers in 1947, reaction in the crowd was mixed. Some people cheered, while others jeered. However, Robinson proved that a mixed-race team could be successful. By the time Jackie retired from baseball in

Jackie Robinson became the first African American to play on a baseball team with people of European ancestry.

1956, after 10 years with the Dodgers, mixed-race teams were appearing in baseball, football, and basketball.

Jackie died on October 24, 1972, following a heart attack.

Poitier Wins Academy Award

In 1963, Sidney Poitier starred in *Lilies of the Field*, a movie about a man who assists a group of nuns in Germany. For his part in the movie, Poitier won the Best Actor Academy Award. He was the first African American man to receive this honor.

Throughout the early days of his career, Poitier broke ground as the first African American actor to win an international film award at the Venice Film Festival, in 1957, and the first African American to become a number-one box office star in the United States, in 1968. Before his Oscar win, Poitier was nominated, in 1958, for his role in *The Defiant Ones*, a film about two escaped prisoners of different races who must learn to work together. This was the first time an African American was nominated for an Oscar. These examples are only some of the many distinguishing moments in Poitier's long and successful career.

Poitier was born on February 20, 1927, in Miami, Florida. He grew up on Cat Island, the Bahamas, where his parents were tomato farmers. Poitier was the youngest of seven children. The family later moved to Nassau, the capital of the Bahamas. This is where Poitier discovered the joys of cinema. When he was 16, he moved

Sidney Poitier starred as Porgy in *Porgy and Bess* in 1959.

Actress Anne Bancroft presented Sidney Poitier with his Academy Award for Best Actor in 1963.

Poitier played a teacher in charge of a rough group of high-school students. *Guess Who's Coming to Dinner* featured Poitier as a young man who meets the parents of his wealthy fiancée, who is of European ancestry. *Guess Who's Coming to Dinner* was the first Hollywood film about a mixed-race relationship that ended happily. It was also the first Hollywood film in which an African American and a person of European ancestry share a kiss.

to New York City. There, in exchange for acting lessons, he worked at the American Negro Theater as an actor.

Following a successful stage career, Poitier made his film debut in *No Way Out* in 1950. Throughout the next two decades, Poitier continued to make movies that challenged **stereotypes**. He sought to play intelligent, complex characters. In *To Sir, with Love,*

In 2001, Poitier's autobiography, *The Measure of a Man,* won a Grammy Award for Best Spoken Word Album. In 2002, he received an honorary Oscar for his long career. Other notable achievements include being appointed a Knight Commander of the Order of the British Empire in 1974 and serving as non-resident Bahamian ambassador to Japan.

African Americans at the Academy Awards

The first African American to win an Oscar at the Academy Awards was a woman named Hattie McDaniels. She received the Oscar for Best Supporting Actress in 1940 for her portrayal of the maid in *Gone with the Wind*. Fourteen years later, in 1954, Dorothy Dandridge became the first African American woman nominated for the Best Actress Award. Although she did not win, her nomination was a notable first.

Since then, African Americans have continued to make their mark in film. Denzel Washington has been nominated for many Oscars. In 2002, he took home the Best Actor award for *Training Day*. That same year, Halle Berry won the Best Actress Oscar for *Monster's Ball*. This was the first time this award went to an African American.

Justice of the Supreme Court

Thurgood Marshall was known for his defense of civil rights and social justice. In 1967, he was made the first African American Justice of the Supreme Court.

Thurgood Marshall was born on July 2, 1908, in Baltimore, Maryland. He encountered racism at an early age, prompting him to fight for African American rights. Marshall applied to study at the University of Maryland Law School but was rejected because of his race. He then applied and was accepted into the Howard University Law School.

In 1933, Marshall received a law degree from Howard University and established a law practice in Baltimore. As a lawyer, he was able to help an African American student named Donald Gaines Murray, who wanted to attend the University of Maryland but could not because of his race. Marshall took the school to court and won, forcing it to admit Murray.

Over the course of his career, Marshall had 29 Supreme Court victories. By 1961, he sought a new challenge. President John F. Kennedy wanted Marshall to become a federal judge. However, all federal judges must be agreed upon by the Senate. In the early 1960s, there were still some senators who did not want to approve

Marshall started working with the Baltimore branch of the NAACP in 1934. Later, he became the assistant special counsel for the NAACP New York City chapter.

Marshall's work to end segregation took him to South Korea and Japan in 1951 to investigate treatment of African Americans by the armed forces. At the request of the United Nations and Great Britain, he helped Ghana and Tanzania draft their constitutions.

an African American judge. They were eventually overruled, and in 1962, Marshall received the Senate's approval.

Marshall's career continued to blossom. In 1965, he was appointed by President Lyndon Johnson to the office of U.S. Solicitor General. Marshall took part in 19 cases on behalf of the government and won all but five. Marshall remained solicitor general until 1967, when he was appointed to the Supreme Court, again by President Johnson. Marshall remained on the Supreme Court until 1991, when he retired.

Marshall died of heart failure on January 24, 1993, at the age of 84. He is buried in Arlington National Cemetery.

Marshall was appointed to the office of U.S. Solicitor General by President Lyndon B. Johnson in 1965.

First African American Astronaut

I n 1967, Robert Henry Lawrence became the first African American astronaut. That same year, he died in a training accident.

Lawrence was born in Chicago, Illinois, on October 2, 1935. In high school, he was one of the top students, graduating when he was 16 years old. After high school, Lawrence studied chemistry at Bradley University in Peoria, Illinois. He received a bachelor's degree in chemistry before achieving a Ph.D. in physical chemistry from Ohio State University in 1965.

Lawrence's military career began while he was still a student at Bradley University. He joined the Air Force's Reserve Officer Training Corps, where he assumed the position of cadet commander. After successfully completing flight training school, Lawrence became an Air Force pilot. In 1967, after further training, Lawrence became a test pilot. He received both the Commendation Medal and the Outstanding Unit Citation from the Air Force.

Lawrence was chosen to participate in the Air Force's Manned Orbiting Laboratory (MOL) program as a test pilot. Although the Air Force and the MOL program were connected during the 1960s, the work of the test pilots was closely related to the work of NASA and its astronauts. In fact, Lawrence's test flights contributed to research on making space shuttles safer.

It was during one of these test flights that Lawrence's fatal accident occurred. He was flying a supersonic Lockheed F-104 Starfighter when he crashed on December 8, 1967. Lawrence was only 32 years old.

Following Lawrence's death, the Robert H. Lawrence Scholarship was set up at Bradley University. In Chicago, Illinois, the Major Robert Lawrence, Jr. School for Mathematics and Science was named in his honor. In 1997, NASA added Lawrence's name to the Astronauts Memorial Foundation Space Mirror.

The Civil Rights Movement

The term "Civil Rights Movement" refers to a series of events that took place between the 1950s and 1960s. The events were a reaction to long-standing discrimination against African Americans and people of other cultures. The movement sought to have people of all races treated as equals. Members of the Civil Rights Movement stood up for their basic rights, including the right to eat, sit, study, and live where they wanted.

Thousands of people took part in the Civil Rights Movement in many different ways. Some people stood out as leaders of the movement. They were the organizers, the spokespeople, and the motivators.

Andrew Jackson Young and Thurgood Marshall are well known for their efforts to promote civil rights. Young helped organize and register voters so that their voices could be heard. Marshall fought and won the historic legal case *Brown vs. The Board of Education of Topeka*. The resulting ruling stated that segregated schools were unconstitutional.

Martin Luther King, Jr.

Rosa Parks

Thurgood Marshall

One of the best-known faces of the Civil Rights Movement was Dr. Martin Luther King, Jr. King was a Baptist minister from Atlanta. When he was 26 years old, he became a symbol of the Civil Rights Movement. He advocated nonviolent protests as a means of creating change.

Another important figure was an African American woman named Rosa Parks, who inspired King to organize peaceful protests. In the 1950s, African Americans could only sit in certain parts of public buses. In 1955, Parks was asked to give up her seat on a bus to a passenger of European ancestry. Parks refused. She had been working all day and was tired. However, because she refused to give up her seat, Parks was arrested.

Many people were outraged by Park's arrest. King encouraged African Americans to stop riding buses. This had an impact on the business as a whole as the fares coming from African American travelers amounted to a substantial part of the transport income. As a result, after a year, buses were desegregated. This was the beginning of King's career as an activist. Although King sought peace, he found violence. Many people opposed the Civil Rights Movement and King's involvement. They threatened him and bombed his house. King continued his movement without fearing for his life. In 1968, King was assassinated in Memphis, Tennessee.

CONTEMPORARY QUICK FACTS

In 1963, Dr. Martin Luther King, Jr. made his "I Have a Dream" speech at Lincoln Memorial. His speech was heard by the millions of people who attended in person or watched him on television. Since then, millions more have heard his inspiring words.

Martin Luther King, Jr. drew strength from other people who protested against racial discrimination, such as Rosa Parks and Thurgood Marshall.

The 1970s

The 1970s built upon the changes of the 1950s and the 1960s. In the 1950s, the **status quo** was challenged. African American writers, actors, and musicians found ways to share their experiences with a diverse audience, and the groundwork for the Civil Rights Movement was laid.

In the 1960s, African American achievements were nationally recognized. Social reform was sought on a number of levels, and many issues were raised. One issue was securing equal treatment for African Americans. Out of this need, the Civil Rights Movement was born, creating waves of change. Segregation ended. African Americans were allowed to vote. They took part in some of the great challenges of the decade, such as the space race.

The radical reforms of the 1960s carried over into the 1970s. The push for more civil rights continued. Women's issues became a hot topic. Space research and exploration continued at a fast pace. Music and art began to change. Many African Americans accomplished remarkable feats in women's rights, politics, and music during this decade.

Stevie Wonder Wins a Grammy

During the 1970s, a musician named Stevie Wonder changed the popular music scene through his creative use of synthesizers and electric keyboards. Wonder's music was met with great success, and at the 1973 Grammy Awards, he was awarded Best Album of the Year. This was the first time this award went to an African American.

Stevie Wonder was born May 13, 1950, in Saginaw, Michigan. He was premature and placed in an **incubator**, where he received too much oxygen. As a result, he lost his sight. Still, Wonder excelled at music and attended school at the Michigan School for the Blind. By 12 years of age, he was given his first record deal, with Motown Records.

Wonder's music during the 1970s was a diverse collection of rock and soul that tackled politics and social issues. In 1976, he signed a $13 million contract with Motown Records, the highest paying record deal at the time. Thirteen years later, Wonder was inducted into the Rock and Roll Hall of Fame. Over the years, Wonder has recorded more than 30 top-10 hits. In 2004, he became the first African American to receive the Johnny Mercer Award in recognition of his successful musical career.

Early African American Concert Singers

African American musicians have contributed a great deal to the music industry. Many have left a lasting legacy.

African American folk songs were popularized and performed by The Hall Johnson Choir in the 1920s. They were organized by Hall Johnson, a violinist. The choir entertained large audiences with spirituals. Spirituals were composed by African American slaves and sung in a hymn-like style. Marian Anderson and Roland Hayes thrilled audiences with soaring operatic arias and music by well-known composers, such as Mozart and Beethoven. Despite the obstacles they faced because of their race, Anderson and Hayes became successful and respected concert singers. Hayes even performed for King George V at Buckingham Palace. Anderson received a Rosenwald Fellowship to study in Europe and was

Roland Hayes

honored by the kings of Denmark and Sweden. The achievements of these musicians helped pave the way for future African American musicians.

Patricia Harris

Patricia Roberts Harris was a champion of social justice and equality. In 1977, she became the first African American woman to serve in a presidential cabinet.

Harris was born in Mattoon, Illinois, in 1924. An excellent student, she attended Howard University on a scholarship. During her years as a student, Harris became a civil rights activist. On one occasion, she participated in a student sit-in in the District of Columbia's Little Palace Cafeteria. The owner refused to serve African Americans, and Harris and the other students staged a peaceful protest in response.

In 1945, Harris graduated from Howard University. For a time, she worked as the Assistant Director for the American Council of Human Rights.

Later, Harris went to George Washington University to study law, where she again proved herself to be the top student, graduating first in her class. Harris went on to argue cases before the United States Supreme Court. In 1965, she was made ambassador to Luxembourg by President Lyndon B. Johnson. She was the first African American woman to become an ambassador. Another first was achieved in 1969, when Harris became the first female dean of Howard University Law School. Eight years later, President Jimmy Carter made Harris the Secretary of Housing and Urban Development. She later

CONTEMPORARY QUICK FACTS

President Lyndon B. Johnson made civil rights a priority during his presidency. He defended the Civil Rights Bill that had been brought to the Senate by his **predecessor**, President John F. Kennedy. The bill said that African Americans must be recognized as citizens and that they had the right to equality.

became the Secretary of Health, Education, and Welfare. As a lawyer and as a member of Cabinet, Harris made a name for herself as a promoter of civil rights and justice. She died of cancer on March 23, 1985.

President Lyndon B. Johnson signed the Civil Rights Act in 1964. This was considered a milestone of the Civil Rights Movement.

U.S. Ambassador to the U.N.

A ndrew Jackson Young is well known as a politician and civil rights activist. His role as U.S. ambassador to the United Nations in 1977 is just one highlight from a distinguished career.

Born on March 12, 1932, Young grew up in New Orleans, Louisiana.

His parents taught him that everyone, regardless of race, deserves to be treated with respect. Young believed that education was a valuable tool. He studied at Howard University in Washington, DC, and graduated with a bachelor of science. Inspired by his faith, Young studied at the Hartford Theological Seminary. He graduated in 1955 with his bachelor of divinity and a desire to teach the world to solve problems peacefully.

Young was very involved in the Civil Rights Movement, and he often worked closely with Martin Luther King, Jr. Young helped in organizing **citizenship** schools for the Southern Christian Leadership Conference (SCLC). These were workshops that taught peaceful protest methods. Young and other members of SCLC helped to register thousands of African American voters in the South. Eventually, Young decided to enter politics, and in 1972, he was elected to Congress. This was the first of three terms Young spent in Congress.

Young was made ambassador to the United Nations in 1977 by President

The SCLC helped people register for voting and pass the voting test. Members included Reverend Jesse Jackson (left), Ralph Abernathy (center), and Andrew Young (right).

Jimmy Carter. Within this role, Young focused on human rights around the world. He was especially concerned with the economies of Third World countries in Africa, and he supported sanctions against **apartheid** in South Africa.

Despite his achievements as ambassador, Young resigned from his position in 1979, after meeting with someone from the Palestinian Liberation Organization (PLO). U.S. officials were not allowed to engage with members of the PLO because it was considered a terrorist organization at that time.

However, Young continued to have a strong political career. He became the mayor of Atlanta, Georgia, in the early 1980s. In 1985, he was re-elected and remained in the mayor's office until 1990. During the 1990s, Young wrote two books, *A Way Out of No Way* and *An Easy Burden: The Civil Rights Movement and the Transformation of America*.

The Southern Christian Leadership Conference

The Southern Christian Leadership Conference was a civil rights organization founded by Martin Luther King, Jr. in 1957. Members of the SCLC believed that peaceful protests were better than violent ones. King believed that "the objective was not to coerce, but to correct; not to break wills or bodies, but to move hearts."

The SCLC allowed King to take his message across America. This was done with the help of workshops that were organized by the SCLC. These workshops taught peaceful protest methods. The organization also helped register thousands of African American voters in the South. The organization intended to draw strength from leaders of the Black Church in the South.

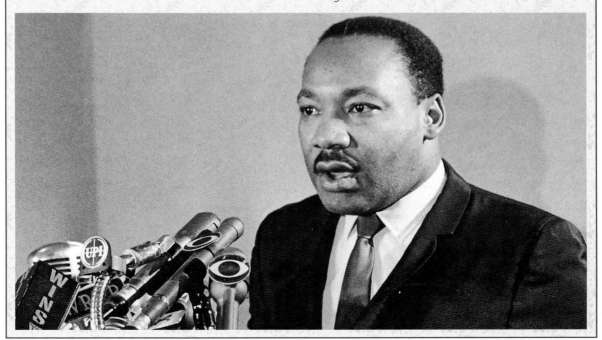

The 1980s

The 1980s are often considered an indulgent decade. During this time, people were very concerned with money. Billionaires and business tycoons became public figures. Shopping was a popular pastime. Media, such as television and magazines, kept track of the wealthiest people in the world.

However, the 1980s were also a decade of exciting advances in technology. People began to use computers in their homes and offices. The cell phone was invented, and advances in medicine were made.

Television audiences were introduced to a new type of show. Team sports continued to grow in popularity. African Americans impacted all of these areas and more.

Guion S. Bluford Reaches Space

The first African American astronaut, Robert H. Lawrence, died during a training accident before he had the chance to travel in space. Sixteen years later, Guion S. Bluford, Jr. had the honor of being the first African American to fly in space. He achieved this distinction in 1983, when he was a mission specialist for a space shuttle flight known as STS-8. This was to be the first of several in-space flights for Bluford.

Bluford was born on November 22, 1942, in Philadelphia, Pennsylvania. By 1978, Bluford had earned his bachelor's, master's, and doctorate degrees in aerospace engineering. In the 1980s, he attended the University of Houston to complete his master's degree in business administration. In addition to these degrees, Bluford has received 13 honorary degrees.

Bluford earned his pilot wings in 1966, after training at Williams Air Force Base in Arizona. An experienced pilot, Bluford logged more than 5,200 jet flight hours and spent 29 years in the U.S. Air Force. During the Vietnam War, Bluford served as a fighter pilot.

In 1979, Bluford joined NASA as an astronaut. This was the beginning of his 15-year career with NASA. His first journey into space, in 1983, was followed by a second flight in 1985 and two more missions in the early 1990s. His achievements as an astronaut were recognized in 1997, when he was inducted into the International Space Hall of Fame.

Following his 1993 retirement from NASA, Bluford embarked on a successful career in business.

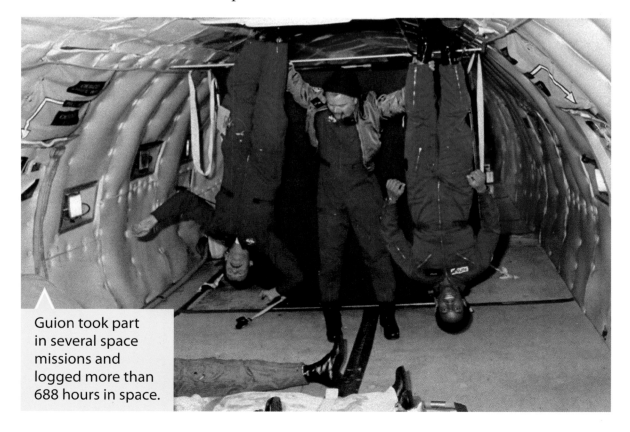

Guion took part in several space missions and logged more than 688 hours in space.

Jordan Joins the Chicago Bulls

Michael Jordan has been called the "best-ever NBA player" and the "most gifted player" by the National Basketball Association (NBA). Among the awards he has won are the NBA Rookie of the Year in 1985 and the NBA Most Valuable Player in 1988. Jordan has made millions of dollars by playing professional basketball and signing **endorsement** deals. Off the court, he has achieved success in commercials and film.

Jordan was born in Brooklyn, New York, on February 17, 1963. His family later moved to Wilmington, North Carolina. Jordan did not attract a great deal of attention for his basketball playing in high school. It was only when he began playing college basketball at the University of North Carolina that he improved his skills and began to achieve recognition for his playing.

In 1997, Michael Jordan helped the Chicago Bulls win the NBA Finals.

In 1984, Jordan was the co-captain of the gold-medal winning United States Olympic basketball team. Many of the best players in the NBA compete on the Olympic team. That same year, Jordan was the third player chosen by the Chicago Bulls in the college draft. This was the beginning of his career as a professional basketball player.

His skill as a basketball player has won him numerous awards and acclaims. He is the first NBA player to win Most Valuable Player awards for the regular season and the playoffs two seasons in a row. In 1992, Jordan again joined the U.S. Olympic basketball team, which won the gold medal.

African Americans in Sports

African Americans have made many contributions to sports. Boxing, golf, tennis, football, and basketball are just some of the sports in which African American athletes have had success. Some African American athletes are well known for their accomplishments as individuals, and others have succeeded as part of a team.

Althea Gibson was a remarkable African American athlete. Born on August 25, 1927, she was encouraged to play tennis as a young girl and soon demonstrated her talent for the sport. A dedicated athlete, Gibson went on to win championships at Wimbledon, the United States Open, and the French Open. In 1957, she became the first African American to be voted Female Athlete of the Year by the Associated Press. After she retired from tennis, Gibson continued to work in sports-related fields. She died on September 28, 2003 of respiratory failure.

Tiger Woods has created a name for himself as a golfer. Woods was born on December 30, 1975, in Cypress, California. He is part African American and part Thai. Even as a young boy, Woods enjoyed golfing. He learned how to play from his father. In 1997, Woods won the U.S. Masters. He was just 21 years old at the time, making him the youngest person to win the U.S. Masters. He also was the first African American to win the competition. Woods has been voted the Professional Golfers Association (PGA) Tour Player of the Year seven

times and won the Arnold Palmer Award eight times. He continues to enjoy huge success on the golf course.

The Oprah Winfrey Show Debuts

P rior to 1986, an African American woman had never hosted a nationally syndicated talk show. That changed with *The Oprah Winfrey Show*, an award-winning program that ran for more than 20 years. Through her show, Winfrey sought to inspire and encourage her audience.

Winfrey has overcome many challenges to become successful. She had a difficult youth, and many people treated her poorly. However, she was a very good student, with many opportunities to advance her education.

Winfrey began her broadcasting career when she was 19 years old as a news anchor at WTVF-TV in Nashville. She was the youngest anchor at the station and its first female African American anchor. After appearing on television in Baltimore, Winfrey moved to Chicago to assume hosting duties on *AM Chicago*. The show became popular, and it was renamed *The Oprah Winfrey Show*. In 1986, the program was nationally syndicated and became a number-one hit. In addition to being the show's host, Winfrey was its supervising producer. The show was produced by Harpo Studios, which is owned by Winfrey, making her the first African American woman to own a media studio. Winfrey purchased the studio to produce movies that she feels have important messages, such as *Their Eyes Were Watching God* and *Beloved*. Winfrey also

Oprah Winfrey donates some of her time and money to many charitable causes.

has a magazine called *O: The Oprah Magazine* and launched a radio show.

For the past several years, Winfrey has been named one of *Time Magazine*'s 100 Most Influential People in the World. She uses this influence to help others. Winfrey supports everyone's right to a good education and has created her own scholarship programs. In 1993, the Oprah Bill was signed into law by President Clinton. This bill, proposed by Winfrey, led to the creation of a database of convicted child abusers.

African Americans on Television

When television was introduced, African Americans were rarely seen on programs. However, in the 1970s, shows such as *The Jeffersons* broke ground by centering on African Americans. *The Jeffersons* featured a hard-working, wealthy drycleaner who moved into a trendy apartment with his wife. The show addressed race-related issues, including multiracial friendships and interracial marriages.

From 1984 to 1992, *The Cosby Show* featured the Huxtables, an upper-middle-class African American family. The show challenged traditional beliefs about African Americans and encouraged friendliness between races. The Huxtables had multiracial friends and respected everyone as equals.

Prior to his success on film, Will Smith was on the television series *The Fresh Prince of Bel-Air.* The show revolved around the Banks, a wealthy, close-knit African American family. The success of the show made Smith a household name. Since then, he has starred in many films, such as *Independence Day, Men in Black,* and *The Pursuit of Happyness.* Before becoming an actor, Smith was a rapper. He and his partner, D.J. Jazzy Jeff, won the first Grammy for rap, in 1988.

The 1970s saw many television shows, such as *The Jeffersons*, that were based on African American families, their lives, and struggles.

The 1990s and Beyond

After all of the advances in technology during the previous decades, the 1990s and 2000s became known as the "electronic age." Cell phones and the internet became essential tools for people to communicate no matter where they were in the world.

Space exploration continued to engage people's imaginations, and scientists began studying Mars. As people became more concerned about the environment, global warming started to draw a great deal of attention.

In politics, the race for the Democratic Party leadership included the first female **candidate**, Hillary Rodham Clinton, and an African American man, Barack Obama.

In recent years, as in the past, African American men and women have demonstrated excellence in the fields of science, art, and politics.

Mae C. Jemison Reaches Space

When Dr. Mae C. Jemison became the first African American woman to travel in space, in 1992, it was a historic moment. Jemison demonstrated that women and **minorities** can be leaders in science and any other fields they choose.

Jemison was born in Decatur, Alabama, on October 17, 1956. However, she grew up in Chicago,

Illinois. In her teens, Jemison attended Morgan Park High School in Chicago, where she was an honor student. In 1973, she graduated from high school, and at 16 years old, she began an **undergraduate degree** at Stanford University.

Following graduation, Jemison continued her studies at Cornell University, where she received a doctorate in medicine in 1981. She decided to use her skills to benefit people living in Third World countries. In addition to working in a refugee camp in Thailand, Jemison visited Cuba and Kenya. Jemison's career as an astronaut began on June 4, 1987, when she was selected for the astronaut training program. After completing her training, Jemison became a mission specialist.

Jemison's first flight into space came on September 12, 1992. She spent eight days in space, making 127 trips around Earth. While there, Jemison conducted research on bone cells.

In 1993, Jemison left NASA. Since then, she has worked as a guest speaker at organizations around the world and appeared on television as the host of the series *World of Wonders*. Jemison also took a job as a teacher at Dartmouth College. She acts as the director of the Jemison Institute for Advancing Technology in Developing Countries. This group looks at ways in which technology might help people around the world.

CONTEMPORARY QUICK FACTS

Jemison took part in a PBS documentary called *The New Explorers: Endeavor*. She also appeared in an episode of *Star Trek: The Next Generation*.

At Stanford University, Jemison studied chemical engineering and African and Afro-American Studies.

Mae C. Jemison became the director of the Jemison Institute for Advancing Technology in Developing Countries in 1993.

Toni Morrison Wins Nobel Prize

A gifted writer, Toni Morrison has received many awards for her fiction. In 1993, she received a special distinction, the Nobel Prize in Literature, in recognition of her outstanding career as an author. Morrison was the first African American woman to receive this award.

Toni Morrison was born Chloe Anthony Wofford on February 18, 1931. She changed her name to Toni, a shortened version of Anthony, while she was a university student.

Even as a child, Morrison showed a love for books. Among her favorite authors were Jane Austen and Gustav Flaubert. Morrison pursued her love of literature as an English student at Howard University in Washington, D.C. Following graduation in 1953, Morrison earned a master's degree from Cornell University in Ithaca, New York, in 1955. She then embarked on an academic career.

While working as a professor at Howard University, Morrison met her husband, Harold Morrison. They had two sons together, and Morrison enjoyed being a parent.

In 1964, Morrison began working as an associate editor for the book publisher Random House. A few years later, she was promoted to senior editor. During this time, she was working on her writing. Morrison would often write at night, once her children were asleep. Her first novel, *The Bluest Eye*, about an African American girl who prays for blue eyes, was published in 1970. It was followed by *Sula*, *Song of Solomon*, *Tar Baby*, *Dreaming Emmett*, *Beloved*, *Jazz*, and *Paradise*. In recent years, Morrison has authored several children's books,

Toni Morrison worked for Random House before her own books were published.

including *The Big Box* and *The Ant or the Grasshopper?*

Morrison is known for the excellent dialogue in her novels and her moving portrayals of African Americans. Her writing continues to affect her readers profoundly.

The Gee's Bend Quilters Collective is Formed

In the small town of Gee's Bend, Alabama, a group of African American women have made a name for themselves as artists because of their skills as quilters. The women of Gee's Bend have been quilting since the 1800s and have developed their own distinct style.

Today, quilting is considered a craft, and quilts are often viewed as pieces of art. The Gee's Bend quilts are examples of modern American art. The Museum of Fine Arts in Houston, Texas, in a partnership with the non-profit group Tinwood Alliance of Atlanta, Georgia, exhibited 70 Gee's Bend quilts in 2002. In 2006, the

museum held another exhibition and tour of the Gee's Bend quilts. As part of the tour, the quilts were showcased at the Whitney Museum in New York, which features only the best examples of contemporary high art. The quilts on display ranged in age. Some dated from the 1920s, while others were recently completed. Both tours were successful, garnering recognition and praise for quilters.

To manage the business of selling their quilts, the Gee's Bend Quilters Collective was formed in 2003. People who buy quilts from the collective can be sure that they are getting an authentic quilt because each quilter signs her finished piece.

Exhibits from Gee's Bend garnered a great deal of praise for its quilters.

Rice Becomes Secretary of State

Condoleezza Rice became the United States' 66th Secretary of State on January 28, 2005 and held the position until 2008. Her swearing-in ceremony was attended by President George Bush. Rice believes that justice and peace should be present in all states and everywhere. As secretary of state, she tried to exercise **diplomacy** while promoting these ideals.

Rice hails from Birmingham, California, where she was born on November 14, 1954. At the University of Denver, she earned her bachelor's degree in political science. This degree was followed by a master's degree from the University of Notre Dame and a doctorate from the Graduate School of International Studies at the University of Denver. Rice is passionate about politics, and her education prepared her for her careers in politics and academics.

In addition to her political roles, Rice is a well-respected professor of political science. She has been a professor at Stanford University since the 1980s and has won two awards. The first was the Walter J. Gores Award for Excellence in Teaching, which she received in 1984. The second is the School of Humanities and Sciences Dean's Award for Distinguished Teaching, which she was awarded in 1993. Rice has a special interest in Soviet political history. Her research has led to several books, including *The Gorbachev Era* and *Uncertain Allegiance: The Soviet Union and the Czechoslovak Army*.

Rice began her political career in the 1980s. In 1986, she was the special assistant to the director of the Joint Chiefs of Staff. Later, she was the senior director of Soviet and East European Affairs in the National Security Council. In 2001, Rice became assistant to the president for National Security Affairs, also known as the National Security Advisor. She held this position until becoming Secretary of State in 2005.

As Secretary of State, Rice was the head of the United States Department of State, which handles foreign affairs matters. She was a member of the president's Cabinet and the highest ranked cabinet secretary, both in line of succession and order of precedence. Her day-to-day work included storage and use of the Great Seal of the United States, performing **protocol**

functions for the White House, drafting proclamations and replies to inquiries, and responding to duties as the president required.

Rice was the National Security Advisor to the U.S. president before she became the Secretary of State.

Barack Obama Runs for President

In 2008, Barack Obama became the first African American presidential candidate for a major party. In January 2009, he became the first African American president.

Obama's mother and father met at the University of Hawai'i. His father, Barack Obama, Sr., was from Kenya but had obtained a scholarship to study at the University of Hawai'i. On August 4, 1961, Barack Obama, Jr. was born. After his father moved back to Kenya, Obama was raised by his mother and his maternal grandparents in Honolulu. He has also lived in Indonesia, New York, and Chicago.

Obama graduated from Columbia University in 1983. Shortly after, he moved to Chicago. Here, Obama spent his time working in neighborhoods where poverty and crime were a concern.

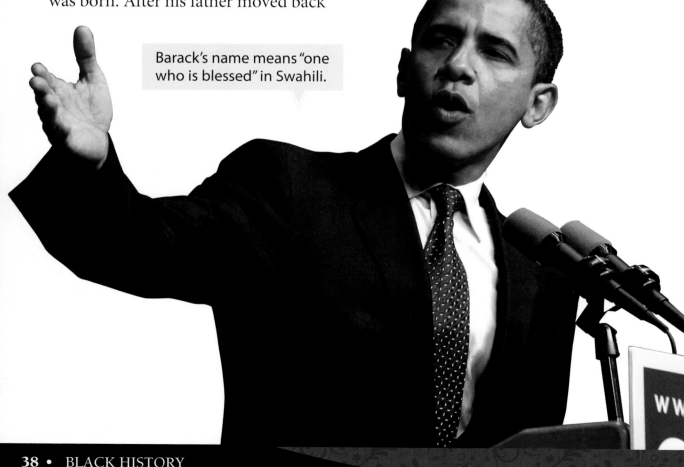

Barack's name means "one who is blessed" in Swahili.

He tried to find ways to improve these neighborhoods. This experience helped Obama realize that, as a lawyer and politician, he could help more people.

Obama returned to university and completed his law degree at Harvard. During this time, he became the president of the *Harvard Law Review*. This was the first time that the *Harvard Law Review* had an African American president. Obama graduated in 1991 and became a civil rights lawyer in Chicago.

Between 1997 and 2005, Obama was a member of the Illinois Senate.

He became a U.S. senator in 2005. As a politician, he has championed the causes of children and veterans, as well as addressing the issues of poverty, the environment, and healthcare. On September 29, 2007, Obama announced that he would run for president of the United States. After a strong campaign, he was chosen as the Democratic candidate. He was elected president in November 2008. Four years later, he was elected to a second term. Obama has said that "people who love their country can change it." Over the years, he has worked hard to create changes for the better.

Michelle Obama

Michelle Obama, Barack Obama's wife, has had a distinguished career. Like Barack, Michelle has touched many people through her work. Michelle was born in Chicago on January 17, 1964. She studied sociology and African American studies at Princeton University and graduated in 1985. Like Barack, Michelle has a law degree from Harvard University. Barack and Michelle met when Michelle was working at Sidney and Austin, a law firm in Chicago.

In 1993, after working for the City of Chicago, Michelle became the founding executive director of a group called Public Allies. This group helps young adults learn professional skills. Three years later, Michelle became the associate dean of student services at the University of Chicago. In 2005, she assumed the role of vice president of community and external affairs at the University of Chicago's Medical Center. As First Lady, Michelle has championed the *Let's Move* program, which encourages children to eat healthy foods and be active.

Continued Success

Throughout history, many African Americans have had to overcome obstacles to achieve success. They have shown great skill, determination, and a willingness to work hard. As a result, they have faced hardships, such as racism and poverty, to fulfill their dreams.

Some struggles can lead to great success, and over the past 60 years, African Americans have accomplished many "firsts." Only a few decades ago, African American athletes could not compete in team sports. Jackie Robinson helped change traditional beliefs when he became a baseball star.

At one time, African American singers could only sing in certain concert halls. Now, musicians such as Stevie Wonder and Will Smith are known for their innovative music skills. African Americans have a strong presence in film and television today. It is difficult to believe that, for many years, African Americans struggled to find their place on screen.

Literary icons, such as Gwendolyn Brooks and Toni Morrison, have drawn on African American history and their own personal experiences to create moving works of literature.

Will Smith has starred in many Hollywood movies including *Men in Black*, *Hitch*, and *The Pursuit of Happyness*.

Successful African American women, such as Oprah Winfrey and Toni Morrison, have helped shape the future of African Americans.

Activists and lawmakers, such as Martin Luther King, Jr., Thurgood Marshall, and Condoleezza Rice, have dedicated themselves to helping others. The research of scientists such as Mae C. Jemison has benefited many people around the world.

Many more African Americans have had great achievements throughout history, and others continue to experience success today.

While some have sought fame, many others have pursued something they felt strongly about. Often, they have used their skills to change the lives of other people for the better.

Timeline

1619: Africans are captured and brought to Jamestown, Virginia, to work as slaves.

1619

1807: Congress declares it illegal to bring slaves into the United States.

1831-1861: About 75,000 slaves escape by the Underground Railroad, a network that helped protect and hide escaped slaves so they could find freedom.

1861: The Civil War begins. One of the main issues behind the conflict is to determine if slavery should be allowed.

1863: President Abraham Lincoln passes the Emancipation Proclamation, which legally frees all slaves.

1865: Congress passes the Thirteenth Amendment, which outlaws slavery.

1866: Congress passes the Civil Rights Act, which declares African Americans as citizens.

1881: The first Jim Crow Law is passed in Tennessee.

1896: In *Plessy v. Ferguson*, the Supreme Court rules that public places may be segregated as long as equal facilities are given to African Americans.

1909: The National Association for the Advancement of Colored People (NAACP) is formed.

1909

1910-1920: During a period known as the Great Migration, about 500,000 African Americans move to northern states.

1861

1914: Marcus Garvey forms the Universal Negro Improvement Association in Jamaica. The group eventually opens branches in the United States.

1919: A series of violent events occur in response to the Great Migration. The period is known as "Red Summer" because of the hundreds of deaths that resulted from the violence.

1942: The Congress of Racial Equality (CORE) is started in Chicago.

1948: President Truman desegregates the army.

1954: In *Brown v. Board of Education of Topeka*, the Supreme Court rules against school segregation.

1955: The Montgomery Bus Boycott begins when Rosa Parks refuses to give up her seat to a passenger of European ancestry.

1957: A community in Little Rock, Arkansas opposes desegregation and plans a protest to prevent nine African American students from entering a school that was formerly for students of European ancestry. The African American students are later called the "Little Rock Nine."

1960: At a Woolworth's lunch counter in Greensboro, North Carolina, four African American college students hold the first sit-in.

1961: The Congress of Racial Equality (CORE) begins to organize Freedom Rides.

1963

1963: Martin Luther King, Jr. writes "Letter from a Birmingham Jail."

1964: Martin Luther King, Jr. is awarded the Nobel Peace Prize.

1965: Malcolm X is assassinated in New York.

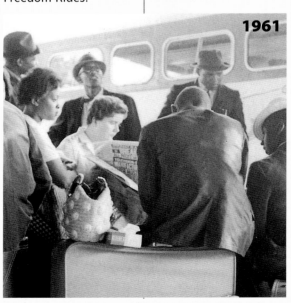

1961

1983: Astronaut Guion "Guy" S. Bluford, Jr., becomes the first African American in space, flying aboard the space shuttle *Challenger*.

1985: Philadelphia State Police bomb a house in Philadelphia occupied by an African American activist organization, MOVE, killing 11 occupants and triggering a fire that destroyed a neighborhood and left more than 300 people homeless.

1986: Martin Luther King, Jr.'s birthday is made into a national holiday.

1989: General Colin L. Powell is the first African American to be named chair of the Joint Chiefs of Staff of the U.S. military.

1989: Oprah Winfrey becomes the first African American woman to host a nationally syndicated talk show.

2008

2008: Barack Obama, a politician from Chicago's South Side, becomes the first African American to be elected president of the United States.

2012: President Obama is elected for a second term.

Activity

What Makes a Leader?

A leader is a person that others can look to as a role model. Leaders have shaped the world we live in. They have changed politics, music, art, and history. In this activity, you will examine what makes a leader.

First, define the word "leader" in your own words. What are some of the characteristics that leaders have?

Next, look up the word "leader" in the dictionary. Compare that definition to your own. What are some of the traits that you missed or included on your list compared to the dictionary?

Now, think about who your role models are. They could be a parent, a grandparent, a teacher, or a celebrity, for example. Write a short paragraph about this leader and why you look up to this person.

Finally, consider some of today's great African American leaders. Choose one, and write a short biography of his or her life. What was his or her impact and what made him or her a great leader?

You will need:

✓ a pen
✓ paper
✓ a dictionary
✓ access to the internet

Test Your Knowledge

1 Who won the Johnny Mercer Award in 2004?

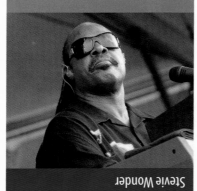

Stevie Wonder

2 Who had published 75 poems by the time she was 16 years of age?

Gwendolyn Brooks

3 Who was originally named Chloe Anthony Wofford?

Toni Morrison

5 Who was the first African American in space?

4 Who spent 10 years playing baseball with the Brooklyn Dodgers?

Jackie Robinson

Guion S. Bluford

6 Who was rejected by the University of Maryland Law School because he was African American?

Thurgood Marshall

Key Words

abolished: put an end to

academics: of or pertaining to colleges, academies, schools, or other educational institutions

activists: people who try to make changes to better the circumstances of a particular cause

apartheid: any system or practice that separates people according to race

Black History Month: a month-long celebration of African American history that takes place in February each year

boycotts: protests in which people refusing to use a public service or purchase goods and services

candidate: a person being considered for a position, such as a job

citizenship: the criteria for belonging to a nation

Civil Rights Movement: a time in U.S. history when African Americans and their supporters fought for equal rights

diplomacy: skill in managing negotiations and handling people

discriminated: treated a person unfairly because of his or her race, gender, age, or physical or mental condition

endorsement: to speak highly of or to promote something

heritage: a person's cultural or historical background

incubator: a heated compartment where babies are sometimes placed for medical reasons

Kwanzaa: a yearly celebration of African American history

minorities: smaller parties or groups that are opposed to a majority

predecessor: someone who has come before

protocol: official standards or rules for government matters

racism: hatred or intolerance of another race

segregation: separation because of race, gender, or religion

sit-ins: organized protests in which protesters sit in one spot and refuse to move

social reform: any type of reform that affects the public

status quo: the existing order of things; present customs, practices, and power relations

stereotypes: widely held beliefs that create a certain image of a person or thing

undergraduate degree: an academic degree that is usually earned after three or more years of college or university study

Index

Log on to www.av2books.com

AV² by Weigl brings you media enhanced books that support active learning. Go to www.av2books.com, and enter the special code found on page 2 of this book. You will gain access to enriched and enhanced content that supplements and complements this book. Content includes video, audio, weblinks, quizzes, a slide show, and activities.

AV² Online Navigation

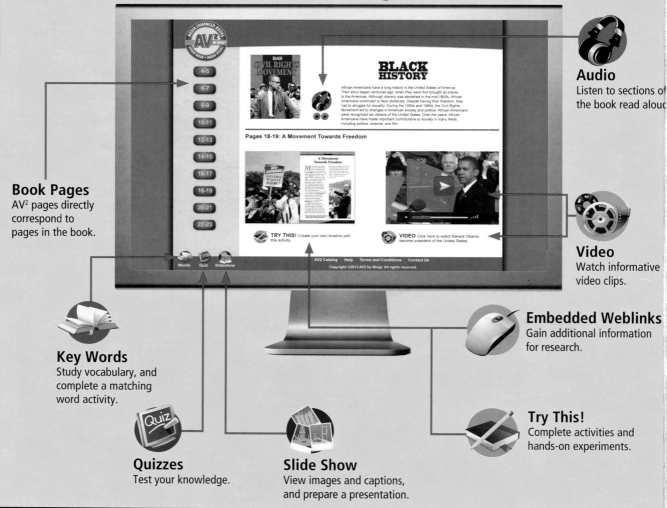

Audio
Listen to sections of the book read aloud

Video
Watch informative video clips.

Book Pages
AV² pages directly correspond to pages in the book.

Embedded Weblinks
Gain additional information for research.

Key Words
Study vocabulary, and complete a matching word activity.

Try This!
Complete activities and hands-on experiments.

Quizzes
Test your knowledge.

Slide Show
View images and captions, and prepare a presentation.

AV² was built to bridge the gap between print and digital. We encourage you to tell us what you like and what you want to see in the future.

Sign up to be an AV² Ambassador at www.av2books.com/ambassador.

Due to the dynamic nature of the Internet, some of the URLs and activities provided as part of AV² by Weigl may have changed or ceased to exist. AV² by Weigl accepts no responsibility for any such changes. All media enhanced books are regularly monitored to update addresses and sites in a timely manner. Contact AV² by Weigl at 1-866-649-3445 or av2books@weigl.com with any questions, comments, or feedback.